Me, Motherhood,
and a
Wise Woman

Me, Motherhood,
and a
Wise Woman

**JULIE WHEATON
& PATRECE POWERS**

SECOND EDITION

FLAMING HOOP PRESS
san diego

Copyright © 2004, 2021 by Julie Wheaton

All rights reserved. Thank you for complying with copyright laws by not reproducing, scanning, or distributing any part of this book without written permission. Brief quotations may be used in book reviews.

Some names have been changed to protect privacy. Book titles and websites mentioned in this book are offered as resources. They do not imply in any way an endorsement by the authors or the publisher. Neither the publisher nor the authors assume responsibility for damages of any kind resulting from the use of the information herein. Trademarks and service marks in this book are the property of their respective registered owners.

Flaming Hoop Press | San Diego, California
FlamingHoopPress@gmail.com

Cover design by Stephanie Hannus | StephanieHannus.com

PUBLISHER'S CATALOGING-IN-PUBLICATION DATA

Names: Wheaton, Julie, author. | Powers, Patrece, author.
Title: Me, motherhood, and a wise woman / Julie Wheaton & Patrece Powers.
Description: Second edition. | San Diego, California : Flaming Hoop Press, [2021] | Originally published as: A fairy godmom's book of reminders. La Jolla, CA : Two Tigers Ink, ©2004.
Identifiers: ISBN 9780984662913 (paperback) | ISBN 9780984662920 (ebook)
Subjects: LCSH: Wheaton, Julie. | Mothers--Biography. | Motherhood--Handbooks, manuals, etc. | Motherhood--Anecdotes. | Mentoring. | Intuition. | LCGFT: Autobiographies. | Handbooks and manuals. | Anecdotes. | BISAC: FAMILY & RELATIONSHIPS / Parenting / Motherhood. | BIOGRAPHY & AUTOBIOGRAPHY / Personal Memoirs.
Classification: LCC HQ759 .W4555 2021 (print) | LCC HQ759 (ebook) | DDC 306.8743--dc23

Contents

1. All Mom 1
2. Crossing Paths 11
3. Playing a Role 17
4. Needs, Wants, and Wishes 25
    Nobody told me it would be like this. 27
    I've never gotten my figure back. 30
    There's so much I don't know about being a mom. 31
    She makes it look so easy. 33
    Maybe I shouldn't have had kids. 36
    How do I get my life back? 38
    People say I'm overprotective. 41
    I'm not the kind of mom I thought I'd be 43
    We need a bigger house. 45
    How can I get my kids to eat well? 47
    I want to give my kids what I never had. 50
    I want more time alone. 51
    I need to get away. 53
    I want more time with my husband. 57
    I want more time with my kids. 60
    I want us to spend more time as a family. 63
    I want my kids to have a pet. 65
    During summer, I feel like an activities director. 67

(Continued on next page)

There are so many unexpected expenses. 69
I can't handle staying home with my kids. 71
I want to be fair to all of my kids. 75
People just don't get it. They don't have *my* kids. 77
I'm uncomfortable with ___, but I don't know why. 78
How can I limit my kids' screen time? 80
I need to mind my own business. 82
I've lost that connection to myself. 83
I feel so responsible for my kids' health. 86
The school system drives me crazy. 88
I can't seem to stop yelling. 91
I feel like I'm being punished for my kid's mistake. 93
I want to be a good role model for my kids. 95
I want to give back for all I've been given. 97
I'm not interested in sex. 99
Maybe I should go back to work. 102
What I see going on in the world scares me. 105
I don't feel ready to have a baby. 106

5. Time Off 107

6. Mindful Mom 113

A Note from Julie and Patrece 119

Acknowledgments 121

Books of Interest 123

Mothers and children evoke something wonderful out of each other.

— PATRECE

- 1 -

All Mom

Before I (Julie) became a mom, my image of pregnancy and motherhood looked something like this: I would glow with natural beauty, I'd wear trendy maternity clothes, and I'd decorate an adorable nursery. I'd have a beautiful, healthy baby (or maybe twins!).

I knew I'd be a good mom because I'd grown up as the oldest of three siblings, and I currently had two dogs. In fact, I'd once had five dogs, and aside from a large bill at the feed store, I managed just fine. Caring for a dog is a lot like caring for a baby, right?

Sure, there was that legendary pain of childbirth, but there was also The Epidural. I'd heard of women who played card games during labor. I could do *that*.

In my image of life as a mom, my husband would be moved by my womanly state. He would work to support our growing family while I'd spend my days cooking healthy meals, making scrapbooks, and dancing my way through the household chores with a baby in tow. No commute to work. No boss. No pantyhose. Just me and my baby going to the grocery store, playing in the park, and blissfully enjoying each other.

— *Screech!!* —

Now here's what really happened: My natural glow was pale green. I was so nauseous for the first three months that I had to hold my breath when I cooked. I craved A&W root beer floats and Orange Julius pizza dogs. I had to pee so often that I confined my fitness walks to construction sites of tract housing because they had Porta Potties.

We lived in a rental house where the "adorable nursery" had rust-colored shag carpeting from 1977. The diaper table was two folded towels covering the entire bathroom counter.

My "trendy maternity clothes" consisted of button-down shirts from my husband, a few borrowed classics from my sister, and the occasional sale item from Target's maternity department. I was determined *not* to own maternity underwear.

One evening, as I changed into my nightgown, my husband looked over at me. I readied myself for a compliment on my womanly state. Instead he blurted out, "What's that on your belly?" I looked down, and there, at waistband level embossed in my flesh, were the words, *Victoria's Secret*. The next day, I went to the maternity store and bought a three-pack of parachutes.

Toward the end of my first pregnancy, I attended the hospital's presentation on pain management. I was horrified by what I saw in movies about the birth process and equally freaked out by the side effects of pain medication. My husband and I went to two classes on natural childbirth but then dropped out after the instructor advised all dads and birth partners to pinch the moms with increasing intensity as a way of simulating labor pains. It felt creepy to have my husband pinching me.

My first labor and delivery experience was straight out of those hospital movies, and I gave birth to a boy. Hours later, I was holding my baby when his breathing suddenly changed. *Is he choking? Is he having a seizure?* I hit the Nurse Call button and studied my newborn for clues. An older nurse wandered in, looked at him, and said plainly, "He has the hiccups."

Upon arriving home, my first order of business was to find loving homes for both dogs. I now knew the difference between pets and people, and my pets weren't ready for little people.

During my second pregnancy, my husband (Michael) and I took weekly classes on natural childbirth, and this time I wrote a birth plan. As I labored in a hospital bed, Michael executed step one of the plan by setting up a boom box to play soothing music. "Turn it off!" I snapped. I needed to focus completely on getting through each contraction. I gave birth to another boy.

Three years later, I had a third boy. In my hospital room, a nurse was examining him when she received an alert on her beeper: another maternity patient had pressed the Nurse Call button. The nurse glanced at the alert, shook her head, and mumbled, "First-time mom."

With each new baby, life was manageable for the few days that my mom or mother-in-law helped. Afterward, it felt like all me, all day at home. I balanced breastfeeding, baby care, and self-care with laundry, bill paying, and grocery shopping. When colic, sleep deprivation, and sickness skidded in, I felt drained and frustrated. Michael was helpful, but as a regional sales rep, he traveled frequently.

At three months of age, our youngest contracted respiratory syncytial virus, or RSV, something I'd never heard of. He was taken by ambulance to the Intensive Care Unit and spent five days in the hospital. Adding to this nightmare was a sudden job layoff weeks earlier. Michael had since found a new job, but it was one thousand miles away. We could only afford to fly him home every other weekend.

There were nights when I was exhausted and alone with my three sons—Big, Middle, and Little—and wondering whether I'd made a horrible choice by becoming a mom. I can remember sitting in a rocking chair trying to comfort a crying baby and finally sobbing myself until I had no energy left to cry.

Whenever I did have a moment to think, my thoughts swirled around the demands of new motherhood. *How was I supposed to take care of a baby, my older kids, and my house at the same time? How was I supposed to "sleep when the baby sleeps" when I was so behind on everything?* Here's a journal entry I wrote shortly after Little was born:

January 19

I feel so overwhelmed. Michael never gets overwhelmed, and this annoys me. He says, "What needs to get done will get done." Intellectually I know this, but everywhere I look in the house I'm reminded of things I need to do. Here's what's on my list today:

- Address birth announcements.
- Send birthday gifts to my niece and 2 nephews.
- Mail back my sister's maternity clothes and the open can of baby formula she left during her visit.
- Plan a birthday party for my 3-year-old.
- Update car insurance with info on new minivan.
- Buy a gift for friends who married 5 months ago.
- Buy 4 baby gifts.
- Take my 11-year-old to buy pants that are only available at GapKids.
- File warranties from Christmas gifts.
- Write Christmas thank-you notes.
- Put away Christmas wrapping.
- Move computer back to Christmas wrapping table.

Other moms would nod when I'd say I was exhausted. Some invited my older kids to play at their homes, and a few offered to take the baby for an hour or two. While I appreciated the babysitting offers, I rarely took advantage of them. It seemed more of an effort to ready the baby for a sitter than it did to care for him myself. Plus, I was uncomfortable accepting help from women who I assumed were busy caring for their own kids. In my world, "busy" was synonymous with "overwhelmed."

Central to my image of being a good mom was being a stay-at-home mom. I also expected to be a room mom, a den mom, and a team mom. I expected to have a clean house and to decorate the boys' bedrooms like ones I'd seen in home magazines. I expected to cook meals from scratch, to throw birthday parties with clever themes, and to head off summer boredom by filling the calendar with movies, crafts, museum visits, picnics, and beach days. I expected to shuttle my kids to extracurricular activities and have their friends hang out at our house.

There's more.

I also expected to stay in good shape, be cheerful, and converse intelligently about current events. I expected economic success, a great marriage, and excellent health.

When I realized that I didn't actually know one person who embodied all of this, I still clung to the idea that someday I'd have it all pulled together, like the other moms I'd seen. If they could do it, I could, too.

In pursuit of being a good mom, I went out of balance. I would react, rather than respond. My behavior was extreme, emotionally driven, and beyond what a situation called for. It was triggered by a variety of external stimuli: kids, extended family members, friends, and the media. At the core was an exaggerated sense of self-importance. I was convinced that I knew what it took to be a good mom. However, while I was doing what it took, I was also losing my sense of self.

I'd felt very responsible for bringing three babies into this world, and I was in a habit of putting all of my energy into being a mom. I reasoned that there would be time for self-development and having a life of my own once the kids were grown. For now, this was my time to be a mom, and I was all mom.

My perspective was so warped that when I met a woman who was traveling with a girlfriend rather than her husband, I assumed she was having marital problems. I asked why her husband wasn't with her, and she said, "We like different types of vacations." At the time, I had no frame of reference for understanding a woman who was creating choices.

- 2 -

Crossing Paths

My firstborn was still a toddler when my then-husband and I divorced. Big would grow up in what the media called "a broken home," and worse, I had broken it. A good mom doesn't do that.

Or does she?

Behind the image was irony. By letting go of my assumption that a good mom stays married for the benefit of her child, I had, without realizing it, taken the first step on a path that would lead to becoming a more authentic and mindful mom.

I put Big into daycare and found a full-time job with a Southern California environmental consultancy. Two months into my new job, the company owner, William, made me an unusual offer: two free sessions with a woman who studies human energy patterns. Her name was Patrece, and she had founded a non-profit corporation dedicated to the study of human energy patterns. William extended this same offer to each new employee out of his belief that the more people know about themselves, the more effective they are at work and in life.

I didn't know what *human energy patterns* meant, but as a single mom navigating so many changes, I welcomed advice from almost anyone. My coworkers had positive things to say about their sessions, so I agreed to meet with Patrece.

On a warm August day, I went to her home office overlooking the Pacific Ocean. A fluffy white dog slept in a sunlit corner while Patrece explained that each of us is born with a unique energy pattern that magnetizes to us various events from which we can learn and grow. No two people have the same pattern, which means that the same event is experienced as something different by each of us. Free will figures into the equation, of course, and in every event, we make a choice to either stagnate or grow.

I found Patrece's work to be so interesting and practical that she and I continued to meet periodically. After I remarried and had Middle and Little, many of my discussions with Patrece revolved around being a mom. She is a generation ahead of me and has a daughter my age.

What I appreciate most is the in-depth and far-reaching nature of what she shares from her training and experience. She doesn't hand me solutions to problems. Instead, she offers a counterpoint to my exaggeration. She reminds me to expand my view and to trust what I know about being a woman, a wife, and a mom.

Sometimes a nudge is all I need to access that higher octave of myself. Other times a good kick in the rear is the kindest way to remind me to act on what I know. More and more, I'm able to catch myself, so I don't have to use huge mood swings or full-blown sickness to get my own attention. I'm learning to replace drama and role-playing with a sense of empowerment that comes from trusting my experience.

- 3 -

Playing a Role

Patrece once said, "Hell has a special place for gushy women." I feel uneasy around a gushy woman because she appears to be playing a role, rather than being herself. But I've also been a gushy woman.

"Playing a role," Patrece says, "happens when a woman acts on images rather than on her natural intuition. Such images are imposed upon us from the media, experts of all kinds, well-meaning family members, and veteran parents. Our values develop and are reinforced as we act on those internal clicks we call 'intuition.' When we observe the results as they pertain to our deep sense of well-being, we can learn more about living from the inside out."

When I try to fulfill external images, I end up feeling unfulfilled and wondering why I don't measure up. Whose yardstick am I using, anyway? When I identify my passions, I become aware of what truly matters to me day by day.

"Each of us is passionate about something," Patrece says. "Imagine living with the courage to make choices that support our satisfaction. Wow! Life now includes us as well as those we love."

When I unconsciously decide that I don't know enough to deal with what's in front of me, I'm tempted to divert my attention to something external, like trends; expert advice; good-mom images; religious, political, or economic doctrine; or some other paradigm that tells me what to do and how to do it. Acting on these images, I might default to playing a role, such as Bossy Woman or Go-with-the-Flow Girl.

As Bossy Woman, I insist on doing everything myself because I'm certain that no one will get it right. Explaining what I need takes too much time, and I have no patience with what I perceive to be incompetence. My kids become overly dependent on me, and my husband probably feels henpecked. I complain about the stress I'm under, but any warmhearted person who calmly suggests that I take some time to rest risks being told that he/she just doesn't understand how impossible that would be. As Bossy Woman, I've been known to do the following:

- Offer unsolicited advice.

- Insert myself into disagreements between others.

- Act as the emotional rudder for those around me. When my young child opens a birthday gift, I shriek, "Isn't that cool?!" Then I write a thank-you note in my child's voice.

- Arrange schedules or set up playdates for kids who are capable of doing so.

- Be overly involved in my kids' homework, club projects, sports, or social life.

- Be outspoken about the standards I have for my family.

- Instruct my husband on how to care for our kids, if I'll be away.

- Overschedule my kids. It's terrific to offer activities that match kids' interests and energy, but talented people don't always discover their passion through after-school enrichment programs. Some discover it during periods of sadness, boredom, or frustration.

As Go-with-the-Flow Girl, I attach myself to others and check with them before making my plans. I put myself last on the list, if I'm on the list at all. I act like my mission in life is to help others, whatever that means at the moment. I use the phrase, "Are you sure?" time and again because I've lost touch with my natural confidence from sacrificing too much of my time and space. I assume that I know how others are feeling, when I don't even know how I'm feeling! I cater to my kids' demands, and my husband is my hero. As Go-with-the-Flow Girl, I've been known to do the following:

- Say yes when I need to say no (and then wonder why I have so little time for myself).

- Use the pronoun *we*, when talking about my kids: "We're teething."

- Do things *for* my kids rather than *with* them. Once the kids lose interest, I do, too.

- Base my decisions on the decisions of others.

- Adhere to tradition or ritual out of guilt. Serving cookies and milk after school is fun, but a ritual done without regard for inspiration or the flow of life eventually loses its luster.

So where's the midpoint between these roles? It's found in honest moments where I take a nanosecond to determine what I need and want from the experience that's directly in front of me. By taking that split second for myself, I can continue to participate in whatever is going on while still tending to my needs.

When I ignore my needs, they don't disappear. They increase. They tug at me, like a child who wants attention: Mom . . . Mom? . . . Mom! . . . MomMomMom . . . *MOM!!!*

Now when I find myself wishing and wanting, I take a small step, even a teeny tiny one, toward what I want. If I want a clean house, I'll take ten minutes to clean one area—not a room, just a corner. If having dinner prepared would make me happy, I'll buy a main dish, a side dish, or a loaf of freshly baked bread.

Patrece asks, "Have you considered that much of what you do for others might be for attention and isn't important to anyone, including you? If what you do *is* necessary, have you considered that *how* you are doing it might be draining your energy? Noticing these subtle yet important questions is as tricky as answering them, especially when we've been entrenched in doing things for others first, last, and always."

If I stay mired in the drama of doing-for-others, what happens when my kids grow up and leave home? Perhaps I'll never allow them to fully leave because I'll need them as my audience. Maybe I'll find other people and places, where I can act out my drama.

Or, I can acknowledge my behavior, separate from it, and reflect on how I used to be. This way, I can continue to reinvent myself by paying attention to my needs, wants, and wishes. I can look for inspiration on the many ways there are to be a woman and a mom. I can choose what to accept with full awareness and what to replace with my own script for individual growth.

- 4 -

Needs, Wants, and Wishes

❖ **Nobody told me it would be like this.**

Why did I expect to be told what it's like to be a mom? Who could have given me an accurate explanation? When I share my experiences with others, do I truly believe that others will have the same experience as I did?

When my sister-in-law was seven months pregnant with her first baby, the doctor ordered bed rest. My sister-in-law was frustrated. She felt fine but was having symptoms that meant something different to her doctor.

"Nobody told me it would be this bad," she said to me over the phone. She asked about my experience with labor and delivery. I shared parts of it, wanting to be truthful, but I was ambivalent about sharing the pain of natural childbirth.

She had heard from other moms that childbirth isn't that hard because of pain medication. She told me she was scared of how medication might affect her baby.

"I understand. I was, too," I said. "For me, natural childbirth turned out to be a worthwhile kind of pain."

Her mother, she said, had an emergency C-section with her first baby.

"What did your mom do then?" I asked. "Did she stop having kids?"

"No," said my sister-in-law. "She had me."

Later, I sent her this note:

> When women share their birth experiences, your feeling of "there's something they're not telling me" is accurate. It's because we can't tell you the whole story. It would be like trying to tell you what your wedding day will be like. When you listen to others' experiences, do you notice how certain parts resonate with you and other parts are forgotten?
>
> You've been pregnant for 7+ months now. How accurately can you describe what it's like to a friend who's never been pregnant? We women are mysterious creatures, and we like it that way. You'll experience childbirth in the same way you've experienced pregnancy: by surrounding yourself with supportive people, trusting your intuition, and being able to laugh at yourself every so often.

Patrece reminds me that, "We can't tell you what it's like, nor should we. If I say 'this is the way it is' and you believe me, then you'll have my experience, not your own. You may have fears and concerns, but which part of yourself do you wish to nurture? All you need is to feel what you're feeling, do what you do, and observe the results.

"What can I offer a woman who's anxious and nervous about pregnancy and childbirth? I can't give her what she's looking for, and she can't get from me what she thinks she needs. Once again, it's the mystery of being a woman.

"Let's enjoy the magical parts that occur unexpectedly and without explanation. There are some things that cannot be explained. Have you noticed that when we try to explain those 'things,' foolishness reigns? That's when we must simply listen. It's the wise person who said, 'Think twice, speak once.' The longer I live, the more I'd like to add, 'Speak once, if at all.'

"Remember how you and I have talked about maturity as a willingness to allow space for ambiguity? We can listen to one another. We can share our presence and value one another's experience without expectation.

"Is a pregnant woman really listening to anyone? The questions she asks are very different from what she wants to know. *Am I going to be safe? Is the baby going to be healthy?* You can reassure her that our bodies are designed for this. It's all make-believe until your body is going through it. It's like when men go off to war thinking they're going to be heroes. Once they get into battle, it's very different than their image. It's a life-altering experience.

"One of the wonders, as we grow older, is to learn the advantages of holding our own counsel. There are things we just don't say because that is how we understand love to be. It's love that creates an atmosphere from our attitudes."

❖ **I've never gotten my figure back.**

Patrece reminds me that, "When you're pulled out of shape, as in pregnancy, you're taking what you have, your body, and making something different with it. Another way to think about it is, once you know something, you can't not know it. And so it is with your body. Once you've had a baby, you can't go back to not having a baby. It's just like everything else in life."

My pregnant sister-in-law asked me about stretch marks and tanning her tummy. I said, "I have a few stretch marks, but I'd forgotten about them until you brought it up just now. For me, stretch marks haven't been a big deal."

Patrece says, "You see? One day it's important, the next day it's not. I think that pregnant women who keep journals will find it most interesting. Your hormones get very bossy. And remember, it's not just pregnancy that has changed you. I know a lot of child-free women who are not at all like they were four or five years ago."

☙

❖ **There's so much I don't know about being a mom.**

I've heard moms who say, "You're only as old as your oldest child." That was true for me. When Big was five, I could recognize and relate to kids who were five or younger, but I felt less confident relating to older kids.

Parents of teenagers would look lovingly at Big and say to me, "You're in the Golden Years, when there's no one in diapers and no one driving. Enjoy it while you can. They grow up fast." I was enjoying this stage, but there was still so much I didn't know about being a mom.

Patrece says, "Admit what you don't know. Saying, 'I don't care' is totally different than saying, 'I don't know.' When you say 'I don't know,' the intent is, 'let's find out together.' Otherwise, there's this conviction that, at some point in life, you're going to know everything, like your mom and dad did, right?" She winks.

Big was twelve when he and I were unpacking dishes from their weeklong stay in moving boxes to put them in the dishwasher. Once the dishwasher was done, Big reached for a plate and said, "Mom, where do the plates go?"

"I don't know," I said.

"Mom, come on! Where do the plates go?"

"I don't know. I haven't lived here before. Where do you think they should go?" Exasperated, he opened a few cupboards, found an empty one, and put away the dishes.

Much like I didn't need to know, ahead of time, where the plates went, maybe I don't need to read up on teenage behavior until I encounter teenage behavior.

☙

❖ She makes it look so easy.

She looks so together.

She has a clean house.

She has a nanny.

She doesn't spend enough time with her kids.

She spends too much time with her kids.

She doesn't need to work.

She is so smart.

She is so creative.

She has a husband who helps with the kids.

She is having an affair.

She volunteers for everything.

She is in great shape.

She is a control freak.

She doesn't even know where her kids are.

For each statement, a different woman comes to mind, proving once and for all that "she" doesn't exist. "She" is a reflection of me. Criticism takes root when I pay more attention to images and concepts than I do to my intuition and to what resonates internally as truth.

Patrece reminds me that, "More often than not, people show us only what they want us to see and tell us only what they want us to hear. We then make comparisons with other mothers, their children, and their lifestyles. However, let's not tire ourselves into believing that we know enough about another to judge who is better than and who is lesser than. We are still getting to know our own mothering ways. We don't know for others."

When I have a strong reaction to a choice that another mom is making, I try to pause long enough to unravel my emotions. *What's missing in my life, such that I feel threatened by a choice she is making for herself?*

Perhaps I lack confidence in an area where she shines. Or maybe, I'm trying to make sense of a choice that wouldn't make sense for where I am right now.

When I'm tempted to criticize, I remind myself that I'm seeing only a slice of another mom's life. (I wouldn't want to be judged solely by some of my slices!) Behind my criticism, I often find confusion. And when I'm confused, it's tempting to focus on something outside myself. When I do that, life sometimes will grant me a set of circumstances similar to the ones I'm criticizing, so I can gain clarity and perspective.

Says Patrece, "Be the woman you are scared to be. You may be doing the same thing as 'she' is, but your intention is different."

ෆ

❖ Maybe I shouldn't have had kids.

"I remember going to playgroups when Betsy was a toddler," said a friend of mine. "I felt so lonesome because everyone just talked about how great it all was. No one ever brought up the difficulties. It feels good just to express that feeling of not always enjoying motherhood."

Patrece reminds me that, "Children need parents to be examples of authentic human beings, people who live as true to themselves as possible. We need that from ourselves, too. Authenticity happens moment by moment, as we give our love and attention to what truly matters to us.

"When we are authentic, children sense in us a certain confidence that comes from an unspoken place. They know they can say something, and we won't take it personally. From day one, children are observing us and learning to survive by understanding what is acceptable or unacceptable.

"Life is not a dress rehearsal. We make our choices, and we live them out. Like one TV commercial says, 'Having a baby changes everything.' Allow those changes to occur. The point of any experience is to cycle through it and integrate what you need from it.

"You wanted children, then you had them, and now you think, *What if I hadn't had children?* You would've missed the experience. The truth is that you didn't want to go on living without having children. Do you honestly believe that, without children, you would've become the same person as you are now? We all change."

❧

❖ How do I get my life back?

After each of my babies, I assumed I'd be the same person I was before. And yet, I knew how I felt around women who had become mothers but seemed determined not to change. Patrece calls this, "extending a role beyond its time."

She says, "Imagine an eighty-year-old woman dressing like a teenager. You've changed. Let yourself play catch-up. Give yourself over to the first three months. Admit you're not the same person you were before the baby and that you won't be ever again and that you don't even want to be. The choice to have a child has permanently changed your life.

"This is not an in-between time from where you were to where you are going. You can't go back to who (you think) you were or forward to who (you think) you're going to be. When you allow yourself to become a mother, growing into and creating a new self, you have a much easier time. You don't come from a place of expectation and demand. Rather, you focus on intuition and observation. In developing awareness, you become more confident.

"Part of the frustration of the first few weeks or months is that you're trying to be a mother as your former self. That self is gone. She has a child now and the choice of growing into a mother or not."

My family and I live in Southern California a few miles from the beach. At first, I blamed our recent move for why I hadn't taken the kids to the beach. We were getting settled, I told myself, and didn't have all of our beach gear organized.

What was truly keeping me from taking three kids to the beach was the preparation involved. I would need to pack a playpen, towels, a beach chair, toys, hats, sunscreen, bodyboards, fins, drinking water, and a cooler with lunch and snacks. To me, all of this effort implied that we should stay at the beach for a while.

Then I realized that we didn't have to stay for long. The kids just wanted to go to the beach. I was applying a mother-of-one approach to a mother-of-three scenario. As a mother of one, I had fewer items to pack, and I could plan around my one child's schedule. As a mother of three, I have more to bring and four people in the comfort equation. Growing into being a mother of three has meant that I'm less attached to outcomes and more aware of doing things for as long as they are enjoyable.

I remember a time when I wanted to exercise first thing in the morning. Michael thought this was a great idea, so he agreed to cook breakfast and get the kids off to school. Our arrangement lasted two weeks, after I started criticizing what

Michael was making for school lunches and pointing out that the kids were going to school in dirty clothes. The truth was I missed seeing the kids in the morning. I returned to my routine with more clarity about how and when I want to participate.

Patrece says, "That's the only methodology we have. Make a choice, and then observe the results in *yourself*—not as an outcome but as how you felt doing it. Do you like yourself doing it?"

☙

❖ People say I'm overprotective.

Five-year-old Middle was jumping into the deep end of a pool, but he was jumping sideways, to keep the edge within reach. "You need to jump farther from the edge," I said as I trailed Little, who was exploring the patio at this apartment complex where my dad lived.

"Julie, he's fine," Dad said. "Why do you have to worry so much?"

Grrr. When people say I worry too much or that I'm overprotective, my initial reaction is defensiveness. "Dad," I said. "If he hits the edge and gets hurt, will he come crying to you or me? I'm the one who will comfort him, drive him to the Emergency Room, wait hours to see a doctor, and pay the bill. I want to prevent that."

I'm speaking from my experience as a mom. I've dealt with stitches, a concussion, injured teeth, and surgery. But I'm also speaking from my experience as a daughter. When I was a kid, Dad would end up in the E.R. occasionally after doing stupid stuff. He once had me drive him to the hospital when I was fourteen.

At the pool, I could have reasoned away my experience and intuition, in order to appear less worried to Dad. But doing so might have put my kids at risk. Instead, I aimed for positive selfishness.

"When people define you," says Patrece, "why not step out of the way and let their label pass you by? Or, if someone calls you 'overprotective' or 'a control freak,' say, 'Thank you for noticing.' If you are feeling overly protective, then consider paying attention with less tension."

∽

❖ I'm not the kind of mom I thought I'd be.

Oh those fabulous and firm ideas I had about parenting before I became a mom! Many of them started with, *No child of mine would be allowed to* _____.

Occasionally, I hear of women who are pregnant with their first child and who have already figured out how being a mom will fit into their lives. Some have arranged for daycare because they are certain they will want to return to work. Others have put their baby's name on the waiting list at what is reputed to be the best preschool.

How many of my pre-mom ideas worked out the way I expected? Very few, if any. Even though I had decided how my life would look with a baby, I was only guessing. What I know for sure is that I signed up for the experience of being a mom, and with each new experience, I know instinctively what I want from it.

Patrece asks, "Do you believe you can choose, ahead of time, the kind of mom you will be, without knowing the specific needs and desires of the child you will be mothering? And equally important, what will you become?

"When you take each experience in its proper sequence, you grow beyond what you ever imagined when you were burdened with preconceptions. Otherwise, there would be no wiggle room for new adventures at home or away."

≈

❖ We need a bigger house.

We need more space. We need a larger kitchen, two home offices, a guest bedroom, and a backyard that's big enough for the kids and their friends. But housing prices here in Southern California have risen faster than our income.

Even though my house and yard feel small right now, I'm realizing how much more relaxed I am when I operate from a base of stability. I like my neighbors in this cookie-cutter subdivision, and we live within walking distance of the boys' schools, the library, and two shopping centers.

Do I really want a guest bedroom? When family members and friends visit, they stay at nearby hotels. I like it that way. It provides privacy and space in our togetherness.

Do I want my kids to change school districts just so they can have their own bedrooms? No. Middle and Little share a bedroom so that I can have a home office. Each boy has a wooden box hidden somewhere in the room, and it's understood that the box is only for its owner to open. Their beds and nightstands are private spaces, too. When I moved past my image that each child should have his own bedroom, I recognized that the boys actually like sharing. For a while, they had their single beds pushed together, and we spent many evenings sprawled out on their big bed reading books and talking.

A larger backyard would be nice, but the kids usually play in the front yard, where their friends are. On any given day, there are six neighborhood kids out there, and groups of teenagers occasionally hang out in our garage.

Moving would require a lot of time, energy, and money. We would need to list our house for sale, keep it clean for showings, pack our stuff, and then fix up the new place so it feels like home. This is the same time and energy I use now to write, to enjoy the outdoors, and to care for my family and myself.

Patrece asks me, "Do you prefer to spend money or buy time?"

⁂

❖ How can I get my kids to eat well?

It's Halloween, a sugar-soaked holiday that isn't my favorite. At Middle's class party, I had to bite my lip when I saw what parents had set out for our kindergarteners:

- Cheetos
- Cracker Jacks
- Cupcakes with green frosting and a cookie tombstone
- Cupcakes with orange and black frosting
- Glazed donuts with colored sprinkles

I resolved then and there to find something healthier for trick-or-treaters. Imagine my delight when I came across a large bag of forty pretzel packages, like what the airlines hand out. I proudly announced to my kids that we'd be handing out something different this Halloween.

"What?!" Big exploded. "Pretzels? Mom, no one likes pretzels for Halloween. That's so lame. No one's even gonna come to our house!" I expected this from a teenager, but when my twenty-four-year-old babysitter said that giving out pennies might be more exciting than pretzels, I re-evaluated.

My continuing interest in healthy eating is a blessing and a curse since I keep raising the bar on what constitutes healthy food. I'd become a frustrated cook because, on most nights, at least one person at the dinner table didn't like what was served.

Around this time, I attended a lecture by a metaphysical practitioner who strongly advised against cooking if you're angry. Food prepared by someone who is angry, he said, is detrimental to the body. These detrimental effects might not show up immediately, but they will show up. He advised staying out of the kitchen, if you're really mad, and instead, going out to eat. He noted that the same principle applies to restaurants. If you sense tension or hear arguing in the kitchen, then leave.

I was reminded of this advice when I first viewed a Kirlian photograph of food before and after it had been blessed. The blessed food glowed with an aura of vitality. When I added that experience to the value I place on organic farming, a new approach to feeding my family began to swirl. It wasn't just what I served but also where the food came from and my attitude in preparing it.

After years of cooking for a family, I was burned out, so I offered each son a night to choose the dinner menu and prepare it with me. For weeks, we ate mac and cheese on Monday, pizza on Tuesday, and tacos on Wednesday. Pretty soon, the kids were also burned out.

From there, we looked for ideas. We morphed fast-food items into healthier fare, we asked grandmothers for family favorites, and we borrowed recipes from neighbors. It was fun to prepare meals *with* my family rather than *for* them.

Patrece reminds me that, "Anytime you think there's a way something should be done, you're working with a fantasy. Does the current condition support your fantasy? If so, it's reality."

She suggested that I put less emphasis on the food and more emphasis on cooking up an atmosphere. I dug out my grandmother's silverware, which had been sitting in a closet for the ten years since her death. Each night before dinner, I turned off the other lights in the house, so the focus was on an inviting table. I served the food family-style, no more deciding who should eat how much of what. I established one rule: You don't have to eat, but you do have to meet. In other words, dinner is about gathering together.

Slowly, I released my white-knuckled grip around the fantasy of an ideal diet, and opted for peace of mind. I love dinnertime now. The kids seem just as healthy, even though we're eating different foods than we used to.

"Healthier, actually," Patrece said, "because of the inviting atmosphere and the companionship."

∞

❖ I want to give my kids what I never had.

Patrece says, "We go to great lengths to fill time and space for our children, as if we need to pour into an empty vessel. However, if we do everything for these little companions, we send the message, 'You can't do this. I have to do it for you. You can't answer that question. I must answer it for you.'

"Children will decide, independent of what was done for them, whether or not they had a so-called 'good' childhood. Over the course of their adult lives, they might even change their minds on this issue several times. While you were growing up, were you aware that your parents were giving you what they never had as children?

"At every phase of their development and ours, we have an opportunity to offer children an example of what it means to be an authentic human being."

❖ **I want more time alone.**

Patrece reminds me that, "Wanting more time alone can also mean that you don't like yourself doing what you're doing. Would you like more time alone or more private time with your family? You can have privacy together. It's a learning curve for most mothers to let family members be alone with them. Privacy doesn't have to be time and space away.

"What invades your privacy? Is it the phone, the TV, or outside noise? If we eliminate what invades our privacy, we can create more space, even with others around. Remember, self-talk also invades your space, and that can be noisier than children's demands for attention.

"A first step toward privacy is recognizing the time that already belongs to you. Maybe you have a few minutes each day, and maybe those few minutes show up spontaneously. Even if they feel inconvenient, practice being aware, and use that time for your benefit. Reflect on what you love about yourself and the new things you're doing as a mom that you never dreamed would be a part of your life.

"Once we discover moments, they overflow into hours. We begin to realize that no one needs our total attention and active participation all of the time. Very possibly it's the need to be needed that keeps us feeling preoccupied with busy-ness."

☙

❖ I need to get away.

Some days, I have two simple wishes: peace and quiet. I took my first soul vacation after fourteen years as a mom. I'd been on trips before but always *with* somebody.

At first, getting away was less of a vacation and more of a desperate act. I saw it as a chance to have a hotel room all to myself. When Michael travels for work, he calls home at night, and our conversation follows an established format: I unload about my day with the kids. He tells me about his day. Then I ask where he went for dinner and what the hotel is like. I envy him for having a hotel room to himself, a gym, and a good meal (prepared by someone else).

So, I outlined three objectives for my soul vacation: I wanted to be able to write, exercise, and eat well. Maybe I'd drive up the California coast and rent a beach house. Maybe I would fly to a city that I'd never visited. But I didn't want to spend a lot of time in transit. I knew I'd be just as happy staying someplace local.

I decided on a week at a health institute thirty minutes from home. I had my own room, and someone was going to make my meals. The institute served a raw, vegan diet designed to detoxify the body.

On day one, I recognized the symptoms of physical detox, but I'd never heard of emotional detox. By day two, the emotional detox was so intense that I drove home and tried to be needed. I told Michael I didn't want to continue the program. He reminded me that he had taken a week off from work to do this. He handed me an apple and sent me on my way.

On day three, a surprise occurred when I called home. Michael went on and on, as though I was the only adult he'd talked to all day. It was nice to discover that this tendency was situational rather than personal.

And what about my secret intent of teaching him a lesson by sticking him with the kids for a week? It backfired. He not only enjoyed his time with the kids but also finished several home improvement projects. (That really got to me.)

I discovered that there's more than just my way to care for the kids. Our parenting styles differ, but our priorities are similar.

Patrece reminds me that, "The more you believe you are needed at home, the more needed you will be, and the more you will want to get away. There's only a need to get away if one has created something that must be escaped. When you go away to write, you like knowing that you have a home to go back to."

"I do," I said.

"Right," she said. "Wherever you go, you still have you."

"Yes, but I'm trying to get away from how I am at home and how I react to my family," I said.

"Right again."

"But even on family vacations, I assume the same roles as I do at home, like activities director and meal planner."

"Yes," she said.

"Yes what?" I asked.

"Just yes," she smiled.

For my next soul vacation, I visited my brother and his wife on a family farm in Idaho. They are a child-free couple in their early thirties. I was visiting, in part, to help with fall harvest. My sister-in-law likes to preserve apples, pears, and plums.

On the ninety-minute drive from the airport to the farm, I asked my brother for a quick course in Houseguest 101, the basics on how our time together could be enjoyable for all. He summarized the course in a sentence: "Just get into your routine as quickly as possible."

So I did. The next morning, I came out in my pajamas, ready to cook breakfast. But no one wanted breakfast. They were doing yoga, making coffee, and gathering items to take to work. I unconsciously followed them around. If one of them went into the kitchen, I went into the kitchen. When they got dressed, so did I. When they sat down with coffee at the kitchen table, I poured myself a cup and sat down, too. I realized the absurdity of my behavior when I nearly followed my sister-in-law into the bathroom.

I kept asking how I could help. They'd glance around the house and shake their heads. Nope, nothing really needed doing. Then I tried to be specific. Could I clean the kitchen? Did the porch need sweeping? Should I start something for dinner? In a moment of enlightenment, I finally said to them, "My behavior will make a lot more sense after you two have kids."

Mama drama can make me feel important and helpful, but it's not the right kind of important and helpful because it's oriented outward.

I shrunk my thinking to fit the situation: I might do the dishes to warm up my hands. It's about sixty degrees in the house. I might cook dinner if I'm feeling inspired. I might sweep the porch if I want to take in some of the crisp air and fall colors. But my motivation will come from within.

℘

❖ **I want more time with my husband.**

My kids and I were picnicking at a grassy neighborhood park when a young couple spread out a blanket nearby and started making out. Awkward. It was a reminder of how oblivious young couples can be when they're in love.

Attempting to recapture this youthful oblivion, I've been known to schedule date night, as if romance needs a regimen. Then, shortly before date night, my attitude takes a nosedive. Sometimes, I can trace the shift to a practical concern, like wanting to avoid the high cost of a babysitter and dinner at a fancy restaurant. Other times, my reluctance is internal. After a long day with the kids, I don't want to dress up and go out.

Patrece says, "Going back to 'the way we were' is an image. We can't go back to that any more than a young couple can advance to where we are. If you hold on to that past image, it's as if being 'in love' is better than the love you now have from the maturity of experience. Just as you were pulled out of shape physically with pregnancy, let love take on a new shape as well.

"As the saying goes, 'A hungry shopper isn't a good shopper.' And so it is with the eagerness and demands in a woman who wants more time with her husband. What is it that you want to share with him? Conversation? Romance? Playtime?

"Your husband is waiting, watching, and wondering. Your task is to recognize how important your attitude is and how it creates what you want the very most and the very least. Once you recognize what a special presence you are, atmosphere follows."

Patrece and I once belonged to a women's group that met each month for a potluck dinner. It was inspiring to see how each woman hosted the gathering in her way. Some women set a few candles on the dining room table; others set candles everywhere. Some played relaxing background music; others played lively music. Because we were a large group, people sat anywhere and everywhere on couches, stairs, and floor cushions.

Patrece says, "The women who hosted the gathering set an atmosphere, not an image. Each of us is born with an aspect of femininity that has never been on the planet before and never will be again. Pay attention to yours.

"Isn't it time to unlearn what we have accepted about femininity that is now unacceptable to us? Pause and ask yourself if the soft, kind, and gentle ways are ones you consider to be less than intelligent, less disciplined.

"Do you know that the word *discipline* is derived from *disciple*? The degree of our devotion is what allows us to be naturally disciplined. Don't you find that the effort goes out of discipline when considered through the looking glass of willing participation?"

☙

❖ I want more time with my kids.

Patrece asks, "What time of day is most enjoyable for you to be with your children? Does this time change according to their ages ... and yours?

"This is about believing that we all have choices. Do you really believe that your children want to be with you all the time? Look again. Be honest. It's humbling, isn't it?

"If you want more time with your children, is it because you think that, when they get older, you're going to regret not spending more time with them? My nephew, Todd, says, 'Regrets are great because they let you live more than one life at a time.'"

Right now, it's 4:30 p.m., and I regret not going to the grocery store earlier. I need food for dinner, but I can't leave now because there are five boys hanging out on our driveway. They're not doing anything special, just enjoying the last few days of summer, and I'd rather be here than at the store.

A few weeks ago, Michael had a similar experience. I asked him to call the boys in, so they could get ready for bed. He walked out the front door but returned too soon. "What happened?" I asked.

He shook his head and smiled. "I can't call 'em inside. They're having too much fun." This time, it was a game of roller hockey. Other times, it's skateboarding on the ramps, rails, and boxes they've built. The activity doesn't matter as much as the flow.

I've interrupted the flow many times, and here's what typically happens: I tell the kids that it's time to go grocery shopping. They whine as they put away their stuff. A neighbor kid can't remember where he left his bike helmet. One of my kids can't find his shoe.

While they clean up, I make a grocery list. That's when the landline rings. Without thinking, I answer it. The boys stand around, glaring at me. They bicker. Finally, I hang up.

At the grocery store, a tussle ensues over who will push the cart. Checkout lines are longer around dinnertime. We arrive home, and I start cooking. Then I remember a main ingredient that I forgot to buy. I call out for pizza.

On this summer afternoon, I know better than to interrupt the flow. I'll come up with something for dinner, even if it's breakfast for dinner. Then I notice a neighbor, Marc, walking towards me carrying a large plastic bag.

In his French accent, he asks, "You guys like pasta?"

"Yes we do," I say.

"Would you like these? They're leftover samples from today." Marc is a caterer.

"Thanks Marc!" I know there's marinara sauce in the freezer and zucchini in the garden.

I wanted to spend this time with my kids more than I wanted to shop for dinner. I took care of myself, and dinner took care of itself.

☙

❖ **I want us to spend more time as a family.**

In my head are images of my family and I trekking Europe, visiting national parks, and camping on the beach. (By the way, my images are free of bad weather, itinerary changes, and sickness.)

So why don't we travel more? Because of a minor point I overlooked in crafting those images: reality. We five have various commitments to work, school, and sports. Plus, the age difference between Big and Little makes it a challenge to find getaways that appeal to everyone.

As I was telling a friend about my wish for more family travel, I realized that the togetherness I equated with travel was occurring at home. Time together creates memories, wherever we are.

Then one summer, we took separate vacations. Michael, Middle, and Little went on a road trip. Big traveled with his grandfather, and I camped on a beach with friends. A week later, we all returned and swapped stories about going to a theme park, bodyboarding in Hawaii, and snorkeling off Catalina Island.

Patrece says, "When everybody goes off in different directions and comes back, you have the whole world to share.

You go be you, and I'll go be me. To do that with children is wonderful. It's life."

※

❖ I want my kids to have a pet.

Growing up, my siblings and I always had pets: dogs, cats, rabbits, fish, pigs, a snake, a rat, and a lamb. I recall feeding the pigs a few times, but otherwise Mom took care of these "family" pets.

Now, I want my kids to have a pet, so they can learn about animals. I want a Labrador, but we have a gerbil-sized backyard. My kids tell me they'd rather have a trampoline than a pet.

"I want my kids to have a pet," I said to Patrece, "but I understand very clearly who will be taking care of it. How do I know if I'm doing this for the right reasons?"

"How do you *not* know?" she asked. "One sure way to know is to trust your experience. Whenever you ask yourself, *How do I know?*, follow it by asking, *How could I not know?*

"We don't want to admit we know because then we're going to be responsible, and we don't want to be responsible for one more thing. The definition I use for *responsibility* is 'response to my own ability.' That takes away the burdened sense.

"The idea is to admit and to trust what you know. Then you can use what you know to find out what you don't yet know. Here's how that works in regard to getting a pet: If you say, 'I don't know,' then there's a tendency to reach outside yourself for the answer. Instead, identify what you do know, and act from there.

"What you know is that *you* will be caring for the pet. Do you have time in your life right now for something more? If you're looking for more time, then why fill up your life with more of anything, pets included?"

ಬ

❖ During summer, I feel like an activities director.

I used to dread summertime. Somewhere along my image-gathering journey, I picked up the idea that a good mom makes sure her kids have a great summer. For me, a great summer means the TV, computer, and video games remain off. For my kids, a great summer means just the opposite.

When I finally retired from my self-appointed position as activities director, the boys were fifteen, seven, and three. Rather than planning my summer around theirs, I decided to plan their summer around mine. I wanted the first two weeks of summer mornings to myself, in order to make headway on a book manuscript.

Big would be on a two-week trip, so I looked for two weeks of half-day camps for Middle and Little. As summer approached, my plan was almost in place, except that I still needed one more week of camp for Middle. Try as I did to find an appealing camp with an opening, it wasn't falling into place, but something else was.

Michael had been laid off after a merger. I assumed that he would have a new job by summertime, but he didn't. So, he offered to be out of the house every morning for a week with Middle, and he asked for ideas on what the two of them could do.

Fortified by this outcome, I set about pursuing my next wish: to read some children's classics. I pulled out my stash of reading lists and showed one to Middle and Little.

"Okay you guys, which books do you want to read from this list?"

Middle stared at me and said plainly, "None of them, Mom. *You* want to read from that list." (Touché Middle.)

At the library, I checked out *Charlotte's Web*. Shortly before the kids' bedtime, I situated myself on the couch and read aloud. No one joined me. The next night, I did the same thing, and the kids snuggled in close.

A few days later, I needed to clear my head after a disagreement with Michael, so I pitched a tent in the backyard and slept outside. The next night, Middle and Little decided to read *Charlotte's Web* in the tent with flashlights. They slept outside for a week. The more I begin with myself, the more I find my kids joining me.

෨

❖ **There are so many unexpected expenses.**

One day, Middle fell on a driveway and suffered a gash to his eyebrow. One of my neighbors, a doctor, confirmed that the gash needed stitches. Because it was a facial injury, the doctor suggested I take Middle to the children's hospital, rather than to the local urgent-care center. At the hospital, Middle and I waited 2½ hours. Prepping and stitching took another ninety minutes. The doctors and nurses were thorough, and they put Middle at ease.

Three weeks later, I received an Explanation of Benefits from our insurance company. The cost for five stitches was equal to our monthly mortgage payment. The situation was ripe for drama. I was tempted to babble about the injustice to everyone or to posture in such a way that others might ask what was bothering me. But I didn't.

I went back to my original intent: the best outcome for Middle. Money hadn't been a consideration then, so why was I now reacting to the cost simply because of a piece of paper that, at the moment, required no action?

I reviewed my past experience with medical bills. Had a doctor or hospital ever submitted an incorrect bill? Yes. Had my insurance company ever processed a claim incorrectly? Yes.

I settled into the comfort of this past experience and waited until action was required. When the bill arrived two months later, our insurance company had negotiated a lower fee, and I was able to finance the balance, interest-free.

ಐ

❖ I can't handle staying home with my kids.

While I'm more confident as the years go by, I've never felt like I'm truly handling it at home. The physical demands of caring for babies and toddlers shift to emotional and mental demands, as kids become teenagers.

After Big was born, I returned to full-time work. After Middle was born, I returned to part-time work. But I disliked putting my kids in daycare because it added a layer of complication to our daily lives. I also felt like I was missing something by being away from my kids for so long. There were qualities I admired in mothers and grandmothers who had stayed home to raise kids, and I wanted to cultivate those in myself. When Big was eight and Middle was four months old, I switched from part-time to freelance work, so I could stay home.

On days when this stay-at-home mom gig is a tough one, I remind myself of something I saw on a church marquee: "Building boys is easier than mending men." As I write this, the boys are sixteen, eight, and four, and I am living for the day when Little starts kindergarten. That will be the first time when all three of my kids are in school for the whole day.

Then, I will finally take time for myself. I'll exercise regularly, keep the house clean(er), and finish all of those projects I've started. I'll read that stack of books I've set aside, and last but not least, I'll return to writing.

But I know better.

This isn't how it will be. If I spend Here wishing for There, then There might not happen the way I am imagining it Here. And if I can't be Here now, how will I ever be There then?

Time to myself is something I want now. If I ignore that desire, I'll continue to be irritated until I take some type of action to let myself know that I'm listening to me. I'm uncomfortable hiring a babysitter for a few hours a week. The cost will strain our already-tight budget, and I'll have to interview strangers and leave my kids with someone I'm not completely sure of.

So, I decide that it's safer and easier to wait until Little goes to kindergarten. That way, I can continue to dream of how great I'll be when I have things my way. Then again, if any of the following scenarios occurs, I might still have someone to care for:

- I could become pregnant again.
- Big could present me with a grandchild.
- A relative or friend could pass over, and I could end up caring for their kids.

- An aging parent could contract a debilitating disease and require caretaking.

My spirit has been nudging me to make incremental changes toward carving out time for myself. Perhaps a high school girl could help me in the afternoons or my sister and I could trade one morning a week of babysitting. Heck, I could go to bed a little earlier and get up before my family. Maybe.

But I'm not committed yet. I still insist on telling myself that I'm doing the right thing for my kids by not hiring a stranger to babysit, no matter how frustrated that makes me. And slowly but surely, I grow more critical of other people, especially moms who take time for themselves.

I drift into mama drama. I want someone to recognize the sacrifices I'm making. Sacrifices are those things that I do but don't really enjoy. And yet, something inside of me is fed by martyrdom. I act angry and overwhelmed. I ignore that small voice inside, even as it repeats its sage advice: *Take one step, and see what happens.* No, I ignore that voice until I am so wiped out that I'm crying daily and hating my life as a stay-at-home mom.

Exhausted, I finally mention to my friend, Alice, that I'm looking for help with my kids. I am richly rewarded for that ounce of courage. Alice says, "I can't believe I've never mentioned Cassie to you. She's our favorite babysitter."

I call Cassie, and she sounds like an ideal match. She arrives at my door, and her enthusiasm washes over my kids and me. They are so taken with her that, as I leave, they barely wave goodbye.

At first, I spend my time on overdue visits to doctors and dentists. Then, I get a haircut. A few weeks later, I go to the library to write. Finally, I push myself to the limit by working in my home office while Cassie plays with the boys downstairs. To my amazement, I write for four hours. Four hours!

With an arrangement that works well for my family and me, I've lost interest in criticizing others. I'm content with what I'm doing. There's no need for external recognition, and there's no sense of sacrifice. Best of all, I'm no longer preoccupied with my perfect, imagined future.

༄

❖ **I want to be fair to all of my kids.**

After I had my second baby, I assumed he'd be much like my first. But I was wrong. Each of my kids has different needs for sleep, food, time with friends, time alone, privileges, and activities.

Patrece says, "The fair thing to do is to recognize those differences, remembering that 'fair' doesn't necessarily imply 'equal.'"

Being fair seems to be a natural outcome of loving my kids equally. But with gift giving, I tend to keep a close eye on cost and quantity, in an effort to be fair. One year, a grandfather in our family announced that he'd be giving gifts only when he felt inspired. Months away from my birthday or the holidays, he'd send a book or a framed photo. Each carried all of the good feelings of a true gift: surprise, delight, and gratitude.

His move away from obligatory gift giving became a hot topic on the family grapevine. Some said that his approach would set up the younger kids in the family for disappointment. I wondered, *Who had set the kids' expectations?* I began to notice how adults would draw the kids' attention to birthdays and holidays with conversations about the gifts that the kids might receive. I'd done this also, to some extent, by asking my kids, nieces, and nephews what was on their birthday or Christmas list.

So, instead of automatically asking for gift ideas, I started by asking myself what type of experience I wanted as a giver. Did I want to shop, make something, or give a gift of time? The more I trusted my intuition, the more I enjoyed the spontaneity of giving from desire rather than duty. I still give according to birthdays and holidays, but my gifts sometimes arrive early or late. Because fairness and equality are values of mine, they influence my gift-giving decisions, but they're no longer a primary focus.

Patrece says, "Once you start living with a modicum of imagination, you will find that keeping score diminishes, as inspiration and desire gain momentum."

༶

❖ **People just don't get it. They don't have *my* kids.**

That's right, and my pity party starts when I feel like no one understands what I'm going through, usually because I'm not getting what I expect, want, or need. Isn't this behavior what I call a tantrum in kids?

Patrece asks, "Why put so much energy into getting people to understand you? Did someone or something get in the way of how you thought things should be, could be, or might be? If the exact same thing worked today, tomorrow, and the next day, we would all be walking around lifeless, rather than as humans being human."

ಏ

❖ I'm uncomfortable with ___, but I don't know why.

When my dad asked if he and his wife could take Little, who was five, to their vacation home for the weekend, my gut reaction was *no*. But I didn't know why. To be polite, I said, "That sounds like fun. Let me think about it." Then I went about the ridiculousness of trying to come up with logical reasons for the way I felt.

The result was a murky mix of facts, observations, and hunches but nothing polished enough to offer Dad as an explanation. So I called around for advice. I called Michael, who was out of town, I called a girlfriend, and I called my sister because her five-year-old had also been invited. Then I called Patrece.

"You just told me that you are uncomfortable with your son going," Patrece said. "That's enough right there, and you may never know why. What matters is *your* peace of mind. You're not comfortable. Period. And it seems that the more reasons you come up, the more uncomfortable you become. I wonder why you reason away your intuition in favor of confusion.

"You have every right as a human being and a mother to say you are uncomfortable with a situation, and therefore you can't participate. First and foremost, say this to yourself. Do you believe it?"

"If it's that simple," I said, "why do I complicate being a mom in so many ways that I drop into bed exhausted on most nights?"

"Hooray!" Patrece said. "When you arrive at the point to ask *that* question, then you can catch yourself before over-thinking or under-feeling."

༄

❖ How can I limit my kids' screen time?

Patrece reminds me that, "Whatever you focus on gives it life. This is a law of physics." If I'm determined to have my kids not watch TV or play video games, then I'm focused on what I don't want. I ran a Nintendo experiment, and here's what I learned: By prohibiting Nintendo in our home, I was drawing the kids' attention to Nintendo. Big kept asking me if he could bring home Grandma's Nintendo. He wouldn't let up, so I gave in and agreed to have Grandma's Nintendo visit for the weekend. The kids were hooked. I'd focused so much on not having Nintendo that it was all they wanted.

Over the years, I've relaxed my rules about screen time. We still don't have Nintendo, and I don't like screen time any more than I used to. But, rather than getting angry or handing out poker chips to the kids so they can buy screen time, I focus on other things. When they ask to watch TV, I ask whether their chores and homework are done. If so, they have free time to spend. In this relaxed atmosphere, TV doesn't have the draw that it once had.

One day, Little came home from kindergarten with a runny nose and looking tired. I said he could watch TV in the family room if he rested on the couch. I rubbed his feet with essential oils, covered him with a blanket, and then went upstairs.

Fifteen minutes later, I came downstairs, and the family room was quiet. I peered in and saw the TV off and Little asleep on the couch. It was the outcome that I had hoped for, but it didn't result from insisting on a nap. It came from setting an atmosphere of relaxation that was more inviting than screen time.

༄

❖ I need to mind my own business.

My friend, Anna, was married to Kyle. Recently divorced, Anna has been negotiating the changing dynamic between her ex-husband and their only child, nine-year-old Jordan.

"I had an epiphany last week," Anna said. "I realized that the farther I stay out of Kyle's orbit, the better. It's taken an incredible amount of emotional and physical energy to play 'clean up' and to ensure that Jordan feels loved and secure. Jordan told me yesterday, unprompted, that she wants to live with me full-time. That may be the right thing, though it makes me sad for her. We'll just have to see. As for me, I am enjoying my new life when I'm not being reactive to Jordan and Kyle's situation."

Patrece likes to say, "To the degree that you ignore your own life, you will insert yourself into the lives of others."

❖ **I've lost that connection to myself.**

When my kids were young, I dreamed of having a few minutes each day to myself. I found those few minutes. Then I imagined having two hours a day. What a luxury! I found that, too. Then I pictured the moment when all three of my kids would be in school at the same time. Surely, I'd finish everything on my to-do list.

That moment has come and gone, and I'm still unable to define exactly what *time to myself* means. I have the time but not the self. I'm busy. Isn't everyone? I'm productive. I cook, clean, drive a carpool, shop for groceries, and pay the bills. I have two freelance projects and a book manuscript in the works.

Perhaps I should re-check the definition of *productive*. I open *Webster's II New Riverside Dictionary* and end up at the root word:

> **pro·duce** 1. To bring forth by a natural process: yield. 2. To bring about: create. 3. To make by a special process: manufacture. 4. To cause to exist: give rise to.

Huh. Where's the part about filling my time with tasks I think I should care about? Maybe I should write *Webster's III New Mom's Dictionary*.

Nothing I'm doing seems, to me, to have the quality of a natural process. I mistakenly believe that what I do is productive because it fills time, and I shudder at the thought of wasting time.

What if I took a minute to define what *productive* means to me? I start by listing all of the things I want to do. What I'm still neglecting though is the quality of those moments. It's not only *what* I do but how I *feel* when I'm doing it. I write because I enjoy it. I stay home with my kids because that's the kind of mom I want to be. I exercise because of how I feel ~~when~~ after I exercise.

I feel most connected to myself when I focus in such a way that time seems to disappear, allowing me to make contact with the quality of the moment. I become aware of myself as a work in progress, as being brought forth by a natural process. I am Webster's incarnate!

Patrece reminds me that, "Any significant change starts with identifying where you are. You know where you are because you know where you've been. Choices begin when you identify what you don't want. From there, it becomes imperative to take some kind of action toward what you do want, to strengthen that connection you have with yourself. Look at your track record. It shows where you've been, and that's what predicts where you are going."

☙

❖ I feel so responsible for my kids' health.

Whenever Big was sick, I would take him to the pediatrician because that's what a good mom does. The waiting room was divided: well kids on one side of the room, sick kids on the other side. The logic reminded me of smoking and non-smoking sections in restaurants and airplanes.

The receptionist would dart around like a hummingbird, answering the phone, signing in patients, and checking out patients. A nurse would take us to an exam room, where we'd wait ten minutes. After a seven-minute visit with the doctor, he'd hand me an antibiotic prescription, and we'd leave. Months later, we'd do the same thing all over again.

When Middle came down with two ear infections before he was four months old, I knew what conventional medicine had to offer. So, I looked for a naturopathic doctor. The idea of strengthening the immune system made sense to me, and I wanted to learn more.

My experience was immediately different. When I called for an appointment, the receptionist was relaxed. She didn't put me on hold three times. The doctor was able to see us that day. In the waiting room, mellow music played. There were plants, a few toys, and a bottled-water dispenser. The doctor met with my whole family for an hour. She asked about diet, sleep patterns, and behaviors. By following her advice and educating myself on alternative treatments, I never again dealt with ear infections.

Still, when my kids would catch a cold or the flu, it was tempting to take them to the pediatrician. But the same thing usually happened. We'd leave with a prescription, and the virus would return a few months later.

Patrece reminds me to, "Keep track of what works and what doesn't. That's an invaluable resource, ready-made for when you need it the most."

I finally learned to trust my experience, but only after one more visit to the pediatrician's office. In the waiting room, I saw runny-nosed kids playing with toys while tired parents gazed at the wall. I heard crying coming from exam rooms. I asked the receptionist if the doctor was running on time. No, she was twenty minutes behind schedule. I cancelled the appointment and took my son to a chiropractor.

These days, I'm less intense about my kids' health. Yes, they still get sick, but by using alternative therapies, we went five years without antibiotics. Patrece once said, "Remember, angels can fly because they take themselves lightly."

☙

❖ The school system drives me crazy.

Big, Middle, and Little attend "good" public schools, even though my definition of "good" has changed over the years. Visits to four Waldorf schools reshaped my ideas on what constitutes a healthy learning environment. In Waldorf classrooms, sunlight and fresh air pour in through open windows. Students are allowed to keep a plant on their desk. Every school has a garden, and larger campuses have farm animals.

Here in coastal Southern California, temperatures are mild, and yet, public schools are built with sealed windows and air-conditioning. Chemical air fresheners and chlorine wipes are commonplace, and hallway vending machines are stocked with sodas and sugary sports drinks.

During one Waldorf tour, a parent asked if the school offered Spanish. An administrator replied, "Yes, we'll offer Spanish as soon as we find a teacher who doesn't use the stickers-and-candy method." At my kids' elementary school, the teachers, counselors, and parent volunteers routinely reward students with candy.

I've searched for schools that better reflect my values. I've looked at homeschooling, and I've calculated the cost of commuting to the nearest Waldorf school. I've considered selling our house and moving to an area where we could live closer to nature.

But I could never come up with a scenario that would also keep the harmony in my household. Tuition for private schooling would be a burden, my kids and I don't have the temperament for homeschooling, and moving out of the area would mean pulling the kids away from friends and most likely a job change for Michael.

"There has to be a different way to educate my kids," I said to Patrece. "But I feel like I'm out of options. I can't find a school that offers affordable tuition, a healthy environment, and hands-on learning."

"There isn't an alternative," she said. "Because every school is part of a system. But you do have a guarantee."

"What do you mean?" I asked.

"It's the atmosphere and values in your home," she said. Patrece, too, had sought out alternatives for educating her daughter. "Julie, the mindset and heart-storming of looking for alternatives is *all* that got me through those years when my daughter was in school. It seemed to me that I tried *everything*. I sent her to four nursery schools because after a few months at each one, she was ready for a change and so was I.

"Thank goodness my husband would remind me, time and again and often when I was in the midst of great angst, that peers, teachers, and conditions at school were paving the way into a world that was going to be much different from ours. I had to take the high road. I committed myself to the task of listening carefully to what my daughter was telling me and showing me about what was going on in her world. It was a show-and-tell assignment: the good, the not so good, and the bad.

"My heart-involved hope was to also show her, by my example, what it meant to think for herself and, at the same time, to do my best *not* to draw conclusions for her. It was a challenging and time-consuming endeavor. In retrospect, it worked!"

I've come to realize that my feelings about the school system, especially as a person outside the system, matter less than how my kids are doing in school. I had to set aside my idealized images and admit that Big, Middle, and Little were happy in public school for reasons all their own. Whenever the school system drives me crazy, I remind myself that school is a microcosm of the world that my kids will navigate as adults.

ಌ

❖ I can't seem to stop yelling.

I once complimented a friend on being a good mom. "I'd be a better one," she said, "if I didn't yell so much. I can't seem to stop yelling."

Lately, most of my yelling occurs at 7:15 a.m. when Little is supposed to be on the sidewalk to catch a neighborhood carpool to school. On days when I drive the carpool, Little's pace is noticeably slower.

"Come on!" I shout, as I head to the front door. "We need to leave now. Let's go! The other kids are waiting!"

"Mom, we don't have to leave this early. All we do at school is wait ten minutes for class to start!"

"But the other kids in the carpool might need more time to get to class!"

"No they don't!" Little shouts. And so it goes, each of us entrenched in being right.

One morning, I was tired of yelling, so I decided to be more self-contained, as Patrece calls it. At 7:10, Little still wasn't ready. To keep my promise to the other families in the carpool, I backed out of the driveway at 7:15, expecting Little to race outside clutching his shoes, lunch bag, and backpack.

He didn't.

I dropped off the other kids and headed toward home, scanning the sidewalk and staying in the left lane in case I would need to make a U-turn to pick up Little. We'd been through this before, and I knew he'd be upset that I'd left without him. I turned onto our street. Surely by now, he'd be on the driveway, fuming.

He wasn't.

I opened the front door, and the house was quiet. Sixty seconds later I heard, "Are you ready, Mom?"

On the drive to school, we made small talk, but neither of us said a word about his being late or my leaving without him. At every intersection, we hit green lights, and Little made it to class on time.

At first, I'd felt smug about being self-contained, but to my surprise, Little had also been self-contained. Each of us had been right about our timing: I needed to leave at 7:15, and he didn't.

∽

❖ I feel like I'm being punished for my kid's mistake.

When Middle was learning to drive, he and I shared my minivan for a year. After Middle got his license, Michael and I bought a third car, so Middle could drive himself to school and sports practice.

A few weeks into having a car, Middle messed up, as teenagers do. I don't recall what he did, but it warranted a consequence. My knee-jerk reaction was to take away his car privileges, even though his mistake was unrelated to the car. The result? I was now driving him to school, sports, and social activities.

I whined to Patrece, "I feel like I'm being punished for his mistake."

"You punished yourself," she said. "You didn't buy a car for your son. You bought a third car as a convenience for yourself. It frees you from having to share your car, and it gives your son what you want for him: safe transportation and a degree of independence. A third car also means you don't have to worry about him bumming rides with friends. Taking away your own convenience doesn't seem intelligent or appropriate to the situation, does it?"

Right again. So I reinstated Middle's car privileges but grounded him. Even though my kids dislike being grounded, it seems to give them a socially acceptable excuse to slow down and disconnect for a bit.

❧

❖ I want to be a good role model for my kids.

Occasionally, I hear a mom who says, "I'm proud of the fact that I work, so my daughter knows she can be more than just a stay-at-home mom."

Patrece reminds me that, "A woman wanting to be a role model is basing her choices on how they will look to others. If we do something to get a reaction, it's manipulative. When we role-play, we act one way while feeling another, again, to get a reaction of some kind. However, there is no guarantee that what we do will impact our children in a favorable way. If you insist on role-playing, then be willing to improvise and turn the page on your script when it's time."

The metaphysical practitioner, mentioned earlier in this book, once talked with me about parents as role models. Having raised eight kids, he said, "Your job as a parent is to establish an image that is really you, not phony. If your kids look at that image and say, 'Oh, that's terrible. I don't want to be like that,' then that's their choice. You set up an image by self-satisfaction, by being the kind of person you want to be. You have to show it in a way that isn't defensive, isn't argumentative, and doesn't push your kids away."

"If you avoid being who you are, the kids grow up role-playing because they see that you're acting. Then you look at them later on, when they're in their twenties, and you shake your head and think, *I can't understand why they're doing that. It's so harmful to them*. Well, you contributed by role-playing. You didn't give them an image of a mother who stays true to herself.

"Why not step out of the role and decide that being you is more important than being Mom? And being you takes care of being Mom."

ೞ

❖ **I want to give back for all I've been given.**

Patrece says, "Giving something because you believe you are Mother Bountiful, and these poor people don't have what you have, is to elevate yourself and discount others. If your intention is to 'take care of those who are less fortunate,' it's time to reconsider. When push comes to shove, each of us finds ways to take care of ourselves with the strength and purpose we once claimed not to have.

"The essence of giving is never about sacrifice. Sacrifice indicates a depletion of energy, as if being martyred. If you 'sacrifice' for your children, how does that feel? Are you implying that sacrifice is a family value? 'Look at all I did for you when you were little, and now that I am older, I need you.'

"All of us have heard this message inferred, if not stated directly. It has nothing to do with the essence of giving. It's bargaining and deal-making.

"How do I know? Because when something is *truly* given, it issues forth from a place that is never depleted. To give a gift of time, interest, or involvement is part of the natural cycle of living. You can check this out for yourself by watching how Mother Nature does it. There is abundance and far more than can ever be used up."

ಲ

❖ I'm not interested in sex.

"If sex feels like just one more thing to do, how did you spend your day?" Patrece asked. "Were you at all aware of moments during the day when it was safe to feel? We are so very overstimulated. What does it mean to be a sensual person? It means something different to everybody."

"But we're conditioned to think of sex in a masculine way," I said.

"Even if we think of sex in a feminine way, there may not be the energy of desire. Thoughts are thoughts, and feelings are feelings. They come from two very different places. To think is not to feel. *I'm not interested in sex* is a thought. *How can I fit sex into this evening?* is a thought.

"*Desire* is such a delicious word. It spills over into everything in life. Imagine losing your taste buds and your desire for wonderful food. Boring! Imagine losing your desire to feel the sun on your skin or resisting the smell of freshly baked bread. It takes a lot of energy to turn off natural delights. What are you resisting? It might be, *I don't want to feel because I'm too busy thinking*.

"Thoughts come and go quickly. True feelings linger much longer. Then you might say, 'I don't have the time to feel.' If we were meant to think more than we were meant to feel, we all would be walking around with huge heads and little bodies.

"Since we are speaking about bodies, loving yours is a silent, undercover job that only you can do. Here we go again, back to the mystery of being a woman. Too much talk, too much thinking about the topic of sex has taken the enjoyment out of the hearts of women.

"There are four basic needs: food, shelter, sleep, and sex. Sex is natural! Ask yourself, *How much of my day is natural?* How many ways can you nurture yourself during the day so that you desire to share yourself, to be enjoyed, and to have pleasure? If a partner's preferences are different than yours, it's going to feel demanding."

"So how do we negotiate preferences?" I asked.

"I don't think sex can be negotiated," she said. "It is to be recognized."

"What's the difference?" I asked.

"When you recognize that one of you wants sexual expression more often than the other, there's the possibility of an acceptance that the rest of the relationship means a great deal. Then you begin to find the interplay of preferences.

"How much separate time do you have, and how do you use it? How much separate time do you trust to one another? People are very afraid about who's going to be attracted to whom. Jealousy and competition consume a lot of energy. When you find people who are relaxed with themselves, you often find people who are relaxed with their sexuality also. An intimate partner once confided in me that he found great pleasure in being with a woman who was relaxed about being a woman.

"What this all comes down to is the passion of living. A little bit of passion carefully distributed over a period of time isn't reasonable. This is about doing what you really want to do, day-to-day. If you say that's a total impossibility when so many demands are being made upon you as a wife and mother, then exciting experiences are needed with a broader perspective that includes being a wife and mother.

"That may sound like so many lovely words packaged into a philosophy for some other time, but you can correct this self-imposed belief if you are willing to identify what life lived with joy looks like to you. Make quick identifications, and once you are willing to do that, your body can tag along for the fun of it."

ༀ

❖ **Maybe I should go back to work.**

I was a college senior when I first encountered Miss Givings. She's the voice in my head that goes around and around, deliberating over past decisions. I'd grown tired of spending my evenings doing homework and studying subjects that seemed irrelevant to my future, so I found a pay phone on campus and called my dad.

"I can't do this anymore. I'm gonna quit school and get a job," I told him.

"Oh no you're not," he said. "You're gonna finish what you started." (I did.)

Now, Miss Givings is ruminating over my choice to be a stay-at-home mom. I hear her say, *It's been great for the kids to have you at home, but is it still the right choice for you?* She yammers on about lost wages, obsolete job skills, and a creeping sense of dependency that comes from relying on a partner's income rather than being a woman of independent means. *Wouldn't you like to be valued for your professional skills and see a paycheck with your name on it?*

Bolstering her position is the fact that Michael and I will soon have eight straight years of college costs for Middle and

Little. Miss Givings wags a figurative finger and says, *That's why you need to go back to work.*

Patrece asked me, "Have you finished what you started? You made a decision to be at home to raise your children. Have you fulfilled your original intention?"

"Not yet. Big is launched, but Middle and Little are still on the launch pad." What Patrece is also asking is if *I* have more to discover about myself through the experience of being at home to raise my kids. Yes, I do.

The kind of mom I want to be moonlights as a writer, not as a mother. A TV interview I once saw sums up how I feel. A famous actress was asked, among other things, how she balanced career and motherhood. Her smile took on a tinge of regret, and she said, "Well, at some point we all stay home to raise our children." She was implying that raising a child to adulthood requires a certain investment of time, energy, and money. She had worked long hours away from home when her kids were young and now found herself parenting an adult child who'd returned to the nest.

To find that shifting midpoint between freelance writer and full-time mom, I've experimented with various locations for my home office: a bedroom, the dining room, a closet under the stairs, my car, and an office park. Then, I had a shed built in our small suburban backyard. The ease of ducking into my shed when I have a slice of free time has kept my writing practice simmering on the back burner. When Middle and Little are launched, I'll turn up the heat.

☙

❖ What I see going on in the world scares me.

The news runs on a continuous loop, 24/7. Sometimes, I create drama by inserting myself into another person's story and using it as my own story. That *is* scary.

But I can't ignore what I see happening.

Says Patrece, "To be defined by the fear of if and when something is going to happen is crazy-making. The news media, along with much of social media, promote those conversations far beyond reason. What is reason-*able*? You are.

"Remember, what is being magnified is being magnified on purpose. Find out what that purpose is, issue by issue, and in that pursuit, you lessen the fear and can enjoy the drama, if that's what you need to occupy your thoughts for the time being. Isn't that what the phrase, *Know thyself,* really means?"

❖ I don't feel ready to have a baby.

My friend, Jan, says, "Maybe it's time that we, as a society, support women if their real choice is not to have kids at all, instead of calling them selfish or incomplete women. We need to support them more fully, so they don't go ahead and have a child or two because that's what is expected. I have three very good friends who've chosen not to be mothers. They contribute substantially to our community and lead very interesting lives. They're some of the most nurturing women I know."

I have a child-free cousin who is a devoted dog mom. One year for my birthday, she sent me a plane ticket to visit her for the weekend. We went on a hike, saw a movie, and toured open houses in a neighborhood where she'd like to live. For me, it was two days of sleeping in, slowing down to a more leisurely pace, and enjoying adult conversation. I came home rested, refreshed, and inspired by what's down the road for me when my kids are grown.

ଛ

- 5 -

Time Off

According to one expert, a stay-at-home mom needs one full day each week to herself. How delightful would that be? The reality is that some moms feel lucky when they can shower alone.

Michael and I have had a rocky start toward giving me time off. He seems to think that if I'm at home, I must be watching the kids. It's my job when he's not around, so why mess up a good thing? My sister and her husband have the same issue. She's figured out that it's better for her to leave the house, if she wants time off, rather than to stick around and risk confusing the kids (and her husband) about who's in charge.

Here's what happened today at our house: Michael had a long lunch break at work, so he came home. He offered to watch three-year-old Little, so I could "take some time for myself." He uses this open-ended phrase to replace more presumptive phrases like, "I'll watch the kids, so you can go grocery shopping" or "I'll watch the kids, so you can go to the gym." *Is he saying I need to go to the gym?*

I told Michael that Little needed a nap. "No problem," Michael said. So, with Michael in charge for the next ninety minutes, I ducked into my office upstairs. Fifteen minutes later, Michael opened my door, popped his head in, and said, "Okay, he's asleep now."

"Great. Thanks," I said and returned to my work, wondering why he'd interrupted me. I don't call him at the office to tell him when Little is napping.

Thirty minutes later, I needed Michael's signature on a form, so I went downstairs. The house was too quiet. I looked in the backyard and then in the garage. No Michael. I walked out the front door, and his car was gone. Apparently, that earlier interruption was code for, "I did what you asked, so now I'm going back to the office." This confusion over who was in charge inspired me to draft some guidelines:

- Guidelines for Mom's Time Off (MTO) -

1. During MTO, you are the responsible parent.

   Even if I'm within reach, you will handle all issues related to poop, vomit, fighting, screen time, food, toys, naps, friends, games, transportation, spills, and breakage of household items.

2. MTO is what it is.

   I might use MTO to go grocery shopping in peace, to enjoy an uninterrupted phone call, or to relax at home while you dance around the demands of our kids. If I do stay home, I will refrain from making critical comments or offering unsolicited advice.

3. MTO may be interrupted for true emergencies.

    Please interrupt MTO for anything involving a hospital, a doctor, or an ambulance.

4. After MTO, there will be a debriefing.

    A quick update from you to me will help us maintain a united front. Please be ready to answer the following questions:

    - Who still has chores to do?
    - Who is where and doing what?
    - Who needs to be picked up and when?

5. I'll take the kids while you tidy up.

    If I return from MTO before you've had a chance to tidy up after your time with the kids, I'll care for them while you do so.

My Promises to You

During MTO, I understand that our kids will be cared for in your way and that household tasks will be handled at your pace. I will avoid commenting on how things should have been done in my absence or what wasn't done at all. I will show my appreciation for you by returning from MTO renewed and happy.

Your Promises to Me

You will schedule time, on a regular basis, to care for our kids and will let me know in advance, so I can schedule MTO.

- 6 -

Mindful Mom

One evening, a new awareness crept up and tapped me on the shoulder. I smiled. Here I was, giving my four-year-old a bath, and for once, I wasn't negotiating when we would wash his hair or telling him what he should do after his bath. I was present and quiet, still and involved. Tears welled up, and I realized that I was beginning to feel again.

I was doing what I'd always done as a mom but with a new intent. I was progressing from mystified and dramatic to mindful and authentic. Patrece reminds me that, "The events in life don't change. We change the way we participate in the events." I was finding new ways to participate:

- Instead of doling out unsolicited advice, I remember that I usually learn more from experience.

- Rather than inserting myself into disagreements between others, I can offer non-verbal assistance, like setting an atmosphere or providing a place to meet.

- I recognize when my kids are old enough to make plans with friends.

- I meld tradition with imagination.
- I say no when I need to say no.
- I enjoy watching my kids discover their interests and abilities in school, sports, clubs, and social activities.
- I view boredom as pure uninterrupted time.
- I understand that silence can be loving communication.
- I ask for help when I need it.
- I take time for myself, without forcing the issue or calling attention to all that I do.

Patrece reminds me that, "Overestimating your need to be needed is a determination you have to make for yourself, especially as a mom. Mothers are among the saints of the world because they really are doing something unnoticed and extremely important. It's up to each one of us to appreciate ourselves."

A Wise Woman

"I woke up this morning," Patrece said, "with this phrase on my mind: chain of command. It related to older women sharing with younger ones. I thought of my mother, who I had less and less in common with as I grew up, but I still treasure many things about her and our relationship.

"The one thing I miss the most is that, whenever I wanted to share something funny, I'd call her, and it became even funnier. We often shared delicious laughter. My women friends who are older than I am offer a perspective with understanding and humor, which seems to come from their experience and self-acceptance."

For me, Patrece has been that older woman friend who shares her wisdom. Her comments awaken in me something familiar yet new. Sometimes, it's her interested silence that helps. Other times, it's her willingness to speak up when I become hardened in my attitudes. In the presence of such an older woman, I've learned to trust my inner wisdom.

For many years, whenever I met with Patrece, I would arrive clutching a list of questions. To my way of thinking, each question represented a separate issue that I was dealing with and which was unrelated to the others on my list.

But as we talked, Patrece would find the common thread that connected my questions. She would show me how they were different aspects of the same pattern. Each conversation with her has felt like a spa for my spirit. And what mom wouldn't enjoy a little more spa time?

❖ A Note from Julie and Patrece ❖

Thank you for reading our book. We invite you to share your thoughts and reactions on Goodreads.com or wherever you like to post reviews.

To purchase the e-book, visit your favorite e-book retailer.

Reach us at …

    julie@juliewheaton.com | mpatrece@gmail.com

❖ Acknowledgments ❖

From Julie:

I am beyond grateful to Patrece for sharing her knowledge, experience, wisdom, and grace.

And although Michael, Big, Middle, and Little are unlikely to ever read this book, I couldn't have written it without them.

From Patrece:

To Julie, my tiger twin, who prowls with vitality, curiosity, and humor in the jungle of life, where gradually revealed to us are reminders to nurture ourselves by following the example of our Mother—Nature.

❖ Books of Interest ❖

Listed in alphabetical order by author's last name.

Phenomenal Woman: Four Poems Celebrating Women
Maya Angelou

The Highly Sensitive Person in Love: Understanding and Managing Relationships When the World Overwhelms You
Elaine N. Aron, Ph.D.

Everyday Sacred: A Woman's Journey Home
Sue Bender

Stop Improving Yourself and Start Living
Roberta Jean Bryant

The Artist's Way: A Spiritual Path to Higher Creativity
Julie Cameron

Parenting with Love and Logic: Teaching Children Responsibility
Foster Cline, M.D. and Jim Fay

Parenting Teens with Love and Logic: Preparing Adolescents for Responsible Adulthood
Foster Cline, M.D. and Jim Fay

God's Dictionary: Divine Definitions for Everyday Enlightenment
Susan Corso

Advice to a Young Wife from an Old Mistress
as told to Michael Drury

Circle of Stones: Woman's Journey to Herself
Judith Duerk

I Sit Listening to the Wind: Woman's Encounter Within Herself
Judith Duerk

The Gift of Story: A Wise Tale About What is Enough
Clarissa Pinkola Estés, Ph.D.

Chop Wood, Carry Water: A Guide to Finding Spiritual Fulfillment in Everyday Life
Rick Fields, with Peggy Taylor, Rex Weyler and Rick Ingrasci

The Book of Qualities
J. Ruth Gendler

Excuse Me, Your Life is Waiting: The Astonishing Power of Feelings
Lynn Grabhorn

The Excuse Me, Your Life is Waiting Playbook
Lynn Grabhorn

A Passion for the Possible: A Guide to Realizing Your True Potential
Jean Houston

Families
Jane Howard

He: Understanding Masculine Psychology
Robert A. Johnson

Inner Gold: Understanding Psychological Projection
Robert A. Johnson

She: Understanding Feminine Psychology
Robert A. Johnson

We: Understanding the Psychology of Romantic Love
Robert A. Johnson

After the Ecstasy, the Laundry: How the Heart Grows Wise on the Spiritual Path
Jack Kornfield

Holy Bible from the Ancient Eastern Text
George M. Lamsa's Translations from the Aramaic of the Peshitta

Kitchen Table Wisdom: Stories that Heal
Rachel Naomi Remen, M.D.

On Becoming a Person: A Therapist's View of Psychotherapy
Carl R. Rogers

The Four Agreements: A Practical Guide to Personal Freedom
Don Miguel Ruiz

The Art of Selfishness
David Seabury

Passages: Predictable Crises of Adult Life
Gail Sheehy

New Passages: Mapping Your Life Across Time
Gail Sheehy

The Art of Growing Up: Simple Ways to Be Yourself at Last
Veronique Vienne

The Art of Possibility: Transforming Professional and Personal Life
Rosamund Stone Zander and Benjamin Zander

www.ingramcontent.com/pod-product-compliance
Lightning Source LLC
Chambersburg PA
CBHW031423290426
44110CB00011B/495